EXTREME DINOSAURS

WORLD'S BIGGEST DINOSAURS

Rupert Matthews

Heinemann Library
Chicago, Illinois

www.capstonepub.com
Visit our website to find out
more information about
Heinemann-Raintree books.

To order:
☎ Phone 888-454-2279
💻 Visit www.capstonepub.com
to browse our catalog and order online.

© 2012 Heinemann Library
an imprint of Capstone Global Library, LLC
Chicago, Illinois

Edited by Rebecca Rissman and Laura Knowles
Designed by Richard Parker
Picture research by Mica Brancic
Originated by Capstone Global Library Ltd
Printed and bound in China by CTPS

15 14 13 12
10 9 8 7 6 5 4 3 2

Library of Congress Cataloging-in-Publication Data
Matthews, Rupert.
  World's biggest dinosaurs / Rupert Matthews.
    p. cm.—(Extreme dinosaurs)
  Includes bibliographical references and index.
  ISBN 978-1-4109-4522-8 (hb)—ISBN 978-1-4109-4529-7
(pb) 1. Dinosaurs—Juvenile literature. I. Title.
  QE861.5.M3743 2012
  567.9--dc23   2011016097

Acknowledgments
We would like to thank the following for permission to
reproduce images: © Capstone Publishers pp. **4** (James Field),
5 (Steve Weston), **6** (Steve Weston), **7** (James Field),
8 (James Field), **9** (Steve Weston), **10** (James Field), **11** (Steve
Weston), **13** (James Field), **14** (Steve Weston), **15** (James Field),
16 (James Field), **17** (Steve Weston), **20** (James Field), **21**
(Steve Weston), **22** (James Field), **23** (James Field), **24** (Steve
Weston), **25** (James Field), **26** (Steve Weston), **27** (James Field);
© Miles Kelly Publishing p. **19** (Rudi Vizi); Shutterstock p. **29**
(© Mark R Higgins).

Background design features reproduced with permission of
Shutterstock/© Szefei/© Fedorov Oleksiy/© Oleg Golovnev/
© Nuttakit.

Cover image of a *Paralititan* reproduced with permission of
© Capstone Publishers/James Field.

We would like to thank Nathan Smith for his invaluable help in
the preparation of this book.

Contents

Some words are shown in bold, **like this**.
You can find out what they mean by
looking in the glossary.

World of Giants

The **dinosaurs** were a group of animals that lived millions of years ago. Some dinosaurs were the biggest animals that ever walked on Earth. *Apatosaurus* was 75 feet long, about twice as long as a bus. The hunter *Saurophaganax* was 36 feet long, more than twice as long as a car.

Saurophaganax

Apatosaurus

Did You Know?
Torosaurus had the largest head of any land animal. It was 8 feet long. That's longer than an average bed!

Torosaurus

African Monster

Sauropods were huge plant eaters with very long necks and tails. One type of sauropod was called *Paralititan*. It was over 85 feet long and weighed about 69 tons. A single bone from its front leg was as long as an adult human is tall. Scientists found **fossils** of *Paralititan* in rocks that used to be part of a coastline. They think it may have swum between islands.

Paralititan

Did You Know?
Paralititan was the largest **dinosaur** to live in Africa.

The Long Neck

One of the longest **dinosaurs** was a **sauropod** called *Diplodocus*. It grew to be 89 feet long. That is longer than the length of a swimming pool. Sauropods lived in herds. The younger animals walked in the center where they could be protected by the larger, older dinosaurs.

Diplodocus

Did You Know?
Some sauropods, such as *Saltasaurus*, had bone **armor** on their backs to protect them from attack.

Saltasaurus

Earth Shaker

Imagine a **dinosaur** so big it made the ground shake when it walked. That was *Seismosaurus*. Its name means "Earthquake Lizard." The **fossil** skeleton was so big it took scientists 13 years to **excavate** all of it.

Did You Know?

Seismosaurus may have been able to make a deafening noise by cracking its tail like a whip.

Horned Face

Ceratopsian dinosaurs were plant eaters with horns on their heads. *Triceratops* was the largest of the ceratopsians. It grew to be 30 feet long and weighed about 4 tons. That is as heavy as an elephant. The three horns on its head were nearly 3 feet long and very sharp. They may have been used to fight off attacks by hunters, such as the *Tyrannosaurus*, shown here.

Triceratops

Old Toothy

Shantungosaurus spent most of its life on all fours, but it could also walk on just its back legs. It was 49 feet long and may have weighed over 16 tons. That is heavier than three Asian elephants. This makes it the largest animal ever to walk on two legs.

Shantungosaurus

Did You Know?
Shantungosaurus had 2,500 teeth in its massive jaws.

Pack Hunter

Dromaeosaurs were hunting **dinosaurs** with large claws on their back legs. *Utahraptor* weighed nearly half a ton. It grew to be 23 feet long, about the same as two dolphins. It may have hunted in packs in order to bring down animals larger than itself. *Utahraptor* was the largest of the dromaeosaurs.

Utahraptor

Did You Know?
The huge claw on *Utahraptor's* back foot was used to kill prey.

Giant Glider

Pterosaurs were flying **reptiles** that had wings of leathery skin. The biggest pterosaur was *Quetzalcoatlus*, which lived in North America about 70 million years ago. It had a wingspan of about 48 feet, making it as big as a small aircraft. Many other pterosaurs were quite small. They had a wingspan of only about 12 inches, the length of a ruler.

Great Bites

Allosaurus was the biggest hunter of its day. It reached about 33 feet in length, nearly as long as a bus. *Allosaurus* had sharp, 2-inch-long teeth that were V-shaped like a saw. The jaws of *Allosaurus* were hinged so that it could gulp down huge lumps of meat.

Allosaurus rests after a big meal

Did You Know?

After a large meal *Allosaurus* may not have needed to eat again for more than a week.

21

Best Crest

Hadrosaurs were four-legged plant eaters who walked on two legs. They often had crests on their heads. The crest was made of hollow bones connected to the nose and may have been used to make loud sounds. *Parasaurolophus* had the biggest crest at about 5 feet long, nearly the height of an adult woman.

crest

Did You Know?

Some scientists think that the head crest may have been used to push tree branches aside as *Parasaurolophus* walked through forests. But nobody really knows for sure.

23

The Great Hunter

Giganotosaurus was the biggest hunter on Earth. It was 43 feet long and weighed nearly 13 tons, so it was about as heavy as 60 lions. The skull of *Giganotosaurus* was the biggest of any meat-eating **dinosaur**. It was over 5 feet long.

Did You Know?

Giganotosaurus may have lived
in family groups. They probably
fought violently over a kill.

Living Tank

Ankylosaurus was the largest of the **ankylosaurians,** or **armored dinosaurs**. It was over 29 feet long, 5 feet wide, and weighed about 6 tons. That is about as heavy as an elephant. The armor covered almost its entire body—even its eyelids were covered by a bony flap.

Did You Know?

Ankylosaurus had a heavy bone club on the end of its tail, which would have been a useful weapon if a hunter attacked it.

club

armor

Studying Fossils

There are many steps to studying **dinosaur fossils**. First, scientists take a photo of the fossil. Then the fossil bones and teeth are fitted together to form a complete skeleton. Often some bones are missing. The skeleton is then used to imagine what the animal looked like when it was alive. Finally the scientist writes a description of the fossils and **publishes** it for others to read.

29

Glossary

ankylosaurians family of armored, plant-eating dinosaurs that lived between 160 and 65 million years ago

armor outer shell or bone on some dinosaurs that protected their bodies

ceratopsians family of horned, plant-eating dinosaurs that lived in North America and Asia toward the end of the age of dinosaurs

dinosaur group of animals that lived on land millions of years ago during the Mesozoic Era. The Mesozoic Era is part of Earth's history that is sometimes called the "Age of Dinosaurs." It is divided into three periods: Triassic, Jurassic, and Cretaceous.

dromaeosaurs family of hunting dinosaurs that were able to run very quickly and had large claws on their back legs

excavate dig something out of the ground

fossil part of a plant or animal that has been buried in rocks for millions of years

hadrosaur family of plant-eating dinosaurs. They are also known as duckbills because many of them had wide, flat mouths that looked like the bill of a duck.

pterosaurs group of flying reptiles that lived between 220 and 65 million years ago

publish print in a book, newspaper, journal, or magazine

reptiles cold-blooded animals such as lizards or crocodiles

sauropods family of plant-eating dinosaurs that had long necks and long tails. The largest dinosaurs of all were sauropods.

Find Out More

Books

Bingham, Caroline. *Dinosaur Encyclopedia.* New York: Dorling Kindersley, 2009.

Lessem, Don. *The Ultimate Dinopedia.* Washington, DC: National Geographic Children's Books, 2010.

Markarian, Margie. *Who Cleans Dinosaur Bones?* Chicago: Heinemann-Raintree, 2010.

Matthews, Rupert. *Ripley Twists: Dinosaurs.* Orlando, FL: Ripley Publishing, 2010.

Websites

science.nationalgeographic.com/science/prehistoric-world.html
Learn more about dinosaurs and other facts about the prehistoric world at this National Geographic Website.

www.ucmp.berkeley.edu/
Learn more about fossils, prehistoric times, and paleontology at this Website of the University of California Museum of Paleontology.

www.nhm.ac.uk/kids-only/dinosaurs
The Natural History Museum is located in London, England. Its Website has a lot of information about dinosaurs, including facts, quizzes, and games.

www.kidsdinos.com/
Play dinosaur games and read about dinosaurs on this Website.

Index